OBSERVATIONS

Books by Idries Shah

Sufi Studies and Middle Eastern Literature
The Sufis
Caravan of Dreams
The Way of the Sufi
Tales of the Dervishes: *Teaching-stories Over a Thousand Years*
Sufi Thought and Action

Traditional Psychology, Teaching Encounters and Narratives
Thinkers of the East: *Studies in Experientialism*
Wisdom of the Idiots
The Dermis Probe
Learning How to Learn: *Psychology and Spirituality in the Sufi Way*
Knowing How to Know
The Magic Monastery: *Analogical and Action Philosophy*
Seeker After Truth
Observations
Evenings with Idries Shah
The Commanding Self

University Lectures
A Perfumed Scorpion (Institute for the Study of Human Knowledge and California University)
Special Problems in the Study of Sufi Ideas (Sussex University)
The Elephant in the Dark: *Christianity, Islam and the Sufis* (Geneva University)
Neglected Aspects of Sufi Study: *Beginning to Begin* (The New School for Social Research)
Letters and Lectures of Idries Shah

Current and Traditional Ideas
Reflections
The Book of the Book
A Veiled Gazelle: *Seeing How to See*
Special Illumination: *The Sufi Use of Humour*

The Mulla Nasrudin Corpus
The Pleasantries of the Incredible Mulla Nasrudin
The Subtleties of the Inimitable Mulla Nasrudin
The Exploits of the Incomparable Mulla Nasrudin
The World of Nasrudin

Travel and Exploration
Destination Mecca

Studies in Minority Beliefs
The Secret Lore of Magic
Oriental Magic

Selected Folktales and Their Background
World Tales

A Novel
Kara Kush

Sociological Works
Darkest England
The Natives Are Restless
The Englishman's Handbook

Translated by Idries Shah
The Hundred Tales of Wisdom (Aflaki's *Munaqib*)

OBSERVATIONS

Idries Shah

ISF PUBLISHING

Foreword

WORDS, THEY SAY, are the food of minds. But, unlike other foods, they can do little by themselves.

Turn words, such as those in this little book of observations, over and over in your own mind, stretching them in all directions, and an alchemy takes place.

Question what you think you know, and what you believe exists, and the answer is likely to be the inverse of what you might first have assumed to be true.

Idries Shah

Someone says that I haven't taught him anything that he can remember. He can't understand yet that that's precisely what I am aiming at...

Lord Wavell, who was once Viceroy and Governor-General of India during the British period, told me that one day an Indian nationalist said to him:

'You British are bandits and yet you accuse us Bengalis of being terrorists. Your official documents even classify some Indians as belonging to "Criminal Tribes"...'

Wavell said, his solitary eye twinkling:

'I simply told the fellow, "Be that as it may – the difference is that *we* are *reformed* bandits!"'

People think that Sufis have too much power because they give orders to people. But they are judging by the false Sufi. Many centuries ago the great Maruf Karkhi of Khorasan put it this way:

'A Sufi has a right to be served, but he has no right to demand.'

Religion is often confused with religiosity, just as it is confused with emotionality and obsession. Spirituality is the essence of religion: and there is, again, an essence of spirituality. Sufism is the essence of essences.

At last it has happened. A research man writes to say that he is preparing a thesis on the 'insusceptibility of Sufi materials to scholarly analysis'.

People confuse behaviour with significance. Quite a lot of approaches to the Sufis are useless; but this is not to say that they may not be elegant and even heroically optimistic – like trying to touch your right elbow with your right hand.

Fame at last. Walking along The Strand in London this dismal, rainy afternoon, I saw a woman with a small boy coming my way on the other side of the street. She said something to him and then ran across the road.

'You're Idries Shah, aren't you?' she asked.

'Yes, I am.'

'Could you please give my little boy some Afghan stamps?'

As quite often happens, a number of people came here today, to discuss what they term the 'difficulties of study'.

We sat through almost interminable accounts of individual problems, personality conflicts, clinical conditions, uncertainties and challenges. I wrote them all down, and was quite easily able to note beside each item a story or teaching which explained the behaviour which was being described.

But when I said: 'I cannot help any of you, because my job is to help people who have taken note of what is already to be noted, which means here people *who do not now suffer* from these forms of self-amusement,' they looked at me with amazement. This is because they read books for what they think they want, not for instruction. All they needed was self-observation and the correcting of wild assumptions, and that is to be found almost everywhere.

The story is told of a man who bought a first-class ticket for a bus journey. Not long after the trip started, he approached the driver and said:

'There are three classes of passenger on this bus. But I cannot see the difference between them. I am a first-class passenger and have paid the highest fare. What do I get?'

'Just you wait and see,' was the only reply he could get.

The bus ground to a halt at the foot of a mountain, and the driver announced:

'Third-class passengers, get out and push. Second-class – walk. The first-class ticket-holders may keep their seats!'

It is bad business practice to manufacture enemies: the world is overstocked with them already.

My first Teacher was asked:

'How can I be less hostile to others?'

He said:

'None can be at all hostile to others unless he or she loves himself, or herself, too much.'

Robert Graves, on seeing a hostile review of one of my books, wrote this to me:

'In case it troubles you, note two things. One, I have had about two thousand worse reviews than you. Two, when you get a bad review, always correct the reviewer's English. For some reason, it is always much worse than that of a real writer.'

Even a hen has a short and flat ruff to sit on, so that it doesn't get in the way. But your mind can be so full of long and short, hard and soft thoughts, that they stick out all over the place, interfering with thinking itself.

Wisdom is when you understand what, previously, at best you only knew.

People try to simplify things beyond the advantage to be gained from so doing. For example, there are times when the *unreasonable* thing to be is reasonable.

Mulla Nasrudin's neighbour had a dog which barked all night.

Nasrudin bought the dog.

'I suppose you're going to get rid of it, Mulla?' asked a crony.

'Not likely! Why should I pay good money and not get my own back? I'm keeping the dog in my own house. Let the people next door find out what it's like to have a neighbour with a barking dog.'

It is said that there are more people trying to study Sufis than there are Sufis to study.

Is this due to a shortage of Sufis?

No, but it does mean that there is a shortage of Sufis available for study.

I asked a television interviewee, much in demand for information on contemporary affairs, to repeat this poem:

'I am now going to my country
    community –
For there I will find knowledge.'
He immediately said:
'At this moment in time
I withdraw to consult my
    Membership
In the grassroots
That's what it is all about.'

One of the great Sufi masters, whom I had asked about the Sufi role in this world, told me:

'If things go wrong, the Sufi is often the person to be blamed. And if the Sufi produces miracles, success, causes an extraordinary and beneficial happening, *this* is attributed by ordinary mankind to mere luck: or its side-issues are pounced on and he is again blamed for them.'

Writers and others know that they are well-known when they are referred to in print and speech without qualification: 'Bloggs says...' is always far more impressive than 'Professor Ralph XYZ Bloggs, PhD, Professor of Cats and Mice at Soanso University, says...'

But beware of thinking that this usage is universal. When a man came to see about the drains here the other day, he said:

'Name of Shah?'

'Yes.'

'I am Mister Bloggs.'

Questions are more important than answers when they make people think. Answers are more important than questions when such answers have no questions.

Sufis restrict their information and actions because to do otherwise would often be both a solecism and absurd: like giving a comb to a bald man.

When something is of interest only to fools, this does not mean that it is intended only for fools.

Not very long ago I was travelling with a renowned sage, learned in the lore of the Far East. When we arrived at Bombay Airport, journalists swarmed on board our aircraft and asked him if he could perform miracles. Our next stop was Cairo, where the information sought was whether he had committed the Koran to memory. Arriving at Paris, the interviewers insisted on being told whether the gentleman had a doctorate in philosophy.

He booked his return flight within the hour after that, and now we shall never see him again.

Have you noticed that when you are wrong, it may only need a child in a crowd to point it out; but that if you are right, it can involve dozens of scholars and decades of work to investigate and vindicate you?

Teaching is like setting bones. In both cases it is not just that something be done, but that it be done correctly and with knowledge. Real teachers spend just as much effort in preventing 'wrong learning' as they do in promoting right learning.

The stationary wheel does not squeak: does not, that is, show its need of lubrication.

A very ugly monkey was throwing stones at the door of a witch with a nasty reputation.

His fellows crowded around to see what would happen.

'Aren't you afraid that she will become infuriated and turn you into a toad?' one asked.

He said: 'That is exactly what I am counting on.'

People who 'disagree with the Sufis' are often found to be thinking along similar lines to those who would 'disagree with the multiplication tables' – because they don't subtract. The Sufis are not there to be agreed with or dissented from. Blake would have understood them: he said, 'Always be ready to speak your mind, and a base man will avoid you.'

The best way to describe people who take pieces of genuine spiritual traditions and use them for emotional or social purposes is to liken this behaviour to that of the man on a sinking ship who found a lifeboat and started to break it up to make the pieces into a raft.

The organisers of a Conference on World Problems were not annoyed because I could not attend. They were, however, infuriated by the fact that I was too busy dealing with the Problems of World Conferences.

Words, they say, are the food of minds.
But, like other foods, they can do little
by themselves.

You think that what the wise have taught about extra dimensions for mankind is absurd. And yet you can conceive that a butterfly which lives only for a day may regard the concept of 'a week' as a ridiculous fantasy.

Sufism is the doing in this lifetime what any fool will be doing in ten thousand years' time.

Three understandings:

There is understanding;
Then understanding of
understanding –
And, finally, the understanding of
what one did not understand.

The second most powerful and effective contribution of the modern world is the healing art brought near to perfection. The first, of course, is the art of destruction.

There is a limit to negligence. You can't forget to die, for instance.

I do not say that the scholars do not know anything about Sufism. You can see from their books that they know all about it – except what it means.

Ignorance is servitude and knowledge gives hope. But only understanding is freedom.

Someone asks why we oppose self-appointed specialists in Sufi matters.

We do not, of course, oppose the method of appointment – only the quality of the appointee...

You say that laughter means superficiality, though you note that lack of a sense of humour is undesirable. I believe that people who appreciate humour are twice as valuable as those who do not. But better still are those who can laugh at jokes and still profit from their serious content.

Self-deception is always very near under two sets of circumstances:

1. When you feel that you are right;
2. When you feel that you are wrong.

It is said that a large enough assemblage of gnats could smother an elephant. Who denies it? But they would, after all that effort, remain gnats.

People are always asking why Sufis are so difficult to find.

Perhaps this is the reason:

It is said that one of the great Sheikhs of Khorasan in olden times decided to walk to Baghdad by easy stages, spending several days at a time in various places en route.

When he started there were very few people on the road; but, as the days passed, more and more people were to be found making their way onto and along the highway.

One day the Sheikh, seeing yet another party flooding onto the road, blocking his path, asked them:

'Brothers, why is the whole world rushing to march in this manner, consuming the world's food and fodder?'

'Haven't you heard?' said the leader of the group. 'The Great Sheikh of

Khorasan is walking to Baghdad, and we thought that there must be some unusual merit in it, so we abandoned our village and are doing the same, following the example of this great man...'

An anonymous reviewer claimed, in a major British literary journal in 1969, that I 'ostentatiously despised' accepted academic behaviour; and published materials showed that this was becoming widely believed during the following two or three years: although the message did not get through to the imitators that the original publication was, by 1971, lauding me for 'opposing pedantry and formalism'.

Then, as the pendulum swung back, my own work was being treated as 'scholarly... impressive, worthy' and so on, and I was showered with invitations to accept professorships. Perhaps this should have restored my faith in academe. But perhaps, again, if the earlier complaints were right that I was a menace to the profession of learning because of my negligence of their standards, I could not do as well as, for instance, Surrey University in granting a BSc degree to a ginger tomcat named Orlando which (according to the *Daily Telegraph*) was enrolled, with professorial approval, in the linguistics department. It is proposed that he should do an MPhil., and that he is considered no ordinary student is evidenced by his candidature for the presidency of the Surrey University Students' Union.

Does this mean that university standards have elevated me, or that they are now on the level of a cat?

The tiniest hurt can produce a thousand curses. But even ten thousand curses cannot make a hole even in a piece of paper.

It is your duty to do your best. It is not, however, your birthright to prevail.

Have you noticed that many people who like to claim that they are suffering from original sin can be seen clearly to be suffering from nothing more original than greed, impatience and laziness?

The gentleman who has just said that he can't understand us because everyone else whom he has contacted in the esoteric sphere regards *him* as genuine, may not realise what sacrifices others may have made to humour him.

The situation reminds me of this anecdote:

A circus-keeper used to show a cage with a lion and a lamb lying down together in it.

Someone (though such people are rare) asked him how he did it.

'Easy!' he answered. 'I just feed lambs to the lion every morning, noon and night, until he can't stand the sight of them.'

If you make friends with a frog, you should prepare for the eagle to be your enemy.

If you wish to be the companion of the bat, you must make friends with the night.

Though you may hate a scorpion, you cannot count on its victims to support you.

A sponge will soak up dirty water as readily as clean: but a person with even a trace of spiritual dishonesty will tend actually to prefer contaminated or useless 'teachings'.

Is the lack of recognition of gold due to the incapacity or negligence of the assessor, or to the nature of the metal itself?

Masses of British and American people, who share, we are told, the same language, clamour for precise definitions of the meanings of Sufi words and phrases.

Perhaps they have not heard of the test in which a group of British and United States citizens were asked which of two definitions of 'a store clerk' was more likely to be the correct one:

(a) Someone who sits in a place where things are brought in, having been sold;

or,

(b) Someone who walks about in a place where things are taken out, having been bought.

All the Americans marked the second version, all the British the first.

I have just been handed a piece of paper with this question on it:

'Why have Sufis all over the world, for centuries, been called liars and opportunists?'

The fact is, of course, that they have far more often, almost always, in fact, been called the reverse.

But assuming that there were some people who felt in this way about Sufis, the answer should be:

'Because the people who said these things could not call the sun "a liar" when it went behind the clouds; or the rain "an opportunist" when it soaked them because they happened to be in the open during a shower.'

Victory over the weak is more shameful than any defeat.

While you are waiting for me to say what, incidentally, I am never going to say, you might as well listen to what I am actually saying.

'A bad teacher,' someone once said to me, 'is no teacher at all. But a bad student – *that* is a disaster.'

Make sure that you really want to learn before you complain of the teaching. Remember the words of St Augustine: 'Make me chaste and continent – but not yet!'

A major purpose of familiarising oneself with Sufi sayings and writings is to acquire a store of statements which can yield their reality at various levels, whose meaning shall be perceived, level by level, when one has almost reached it, so that this meaning helps one to rise further.

Say what you should not, and you will
have to hear what you would not.

They say that people will think a fool wise if he does not speak. But if he is a fool, is he likely to act upon the suggestion?

A young Western Seeker-after-Truth has just returned from one of the usual, well-meant but almost useless journeys with which such people amuse themselves. He did, however, notice something which is worth noting, though he spent far too much time and money learning it. This is what he said, somewhat abbreviated:

'When I looked for goulash in Hungary, I found that this meant not stew but soup. What *we* call "goulash", they called "pörköltt" – and that can be made of fish, not beef as we do. In Pakistan, "Tandoori" merely means "from the oven", and the Chinese laughed when I asked for "Chop-Suey", since, far from being a delicacy, it means, "scraps and odds and ends", they say. In India, when I asked for spirituality, even from greatly revered gurus, all I got was rehashed sentimentality which was quite insipid. I wonder what one has to ask for there, and how, in order to get the real thing?'

People haven't changed in the centuries since the Master Saadi said:

'Not a trifling word is said to the master of awareness but he will grasp its wisdom; and if a hundred chapters of wisdom are read in the presence of an ignorant one – it will all reach his ears as a trifle.'

If you wish to meet yourself, observe your thoughts and reactions under unusual circumstances.

Truth is hateful to the hypocrite; but you must find a way to introduce it under his guard. Because this is so difficult, masses of hypocrites are undetected, especially by themselves.

You don't have to know everything to
be wise:
    You don't have to know everyone to
be valued.

If I say 'The sun is shining', everyone knows what I mean.

That is, they think that they do. Few, however, will realise when they hear that phrase that the sun is always shining and that what makes it appear that it is not is the clouds which are interposed between it and us.

For some purposes it does not matter whether we know or take note of the facts about the weather. For others it could make a very great difference.

If it is to make the difference for us, we have to know it and to register it.

The same principle holds good with respect to Sufism and ultimate Reality.

All I can say about the man to whom you have just referred is that he is the sort of man who would go to England because of the weather...

I once asked a very wise man how he had developed the power of seeing through hypocrites and frauds; how it was that his assessments of people were so uncannily accurate.

He said:

'Most people listen to talk and mix hearsay and repute with it. All *I* do is to stop listening... I watch!'

It is easy to make hopes come true: just live up to someone's expectations of you.

People are always asking why they do not make more progress in their inward studies.

The answer is simple for the detached observer.

You cannot keep a crow and corn in the same field, when the crow is hungry and the corn is sparse.

Can you approach Truth, do you think, if you cannot be honest about your own dishonesty?

The moment you are born, you become a moving target for the world. You may be much more than this, but do you remember that you are a target as well?

Are you ignorant enough to expect horsemanship from blacksmiths?

People are always asking why we do not seek truth through the relics and records which are so abundant.

They are, of course, people who forget that if you plant cheese you will not harvest milk.

Wisdom gives honour to nobility, and nobility to everything else.

If you want to nourish your stupidity, try a little avarice.

Education has its problems. This includes making the wise wiser and the foolish more foolish.

As the air does not exist to be looked at, the Sufis do not exist except for practice. They do not exist for discussion.

The imagination of the wise is truer than the knowledge of fools.

Some years ago I was asked on a radio programme why, in a certain book which I had written, the Sufis always 'came out on top'. Why did they never come unstuck, he wanted to know.

I was at first surprised at such a prominent individual as my interviewer asking a question like that when he could have thought out the answer for himself; but I assumed that it was rhetorical, and that he was giving me an opportunity of explaining for the duller listeners, that the material was instructional, like a book of mathematical tables.

The other day I met a well-known scholar for the first time. As soon as we were introduced, he said:

'Chap interviewing you on the radio once made a telling point against you about Sufis always coming out on top. I noticed that you dodged the issue, but I couldn't help noticing that you had no answer!'

Just as some Western techniques and instruments of great promise, indiscriminately introduced and carelessly used, have harmed people in the East, so does the random and incomplete importation of Eastern ideas and practices often act adversely on people of the West.

Listen to advice based on experience; it cost a great deal, but you are not charged for it. Yet the payment which you should make is to try to understand it.

Claiming that anyone can get anywhere will get you anywhere in most human communities. What is perhaps worthy of remark, however, is that this will not get those communities anywhere.

The knowledge of those without depth
is like poor cloth – put a patch on it
here and a rent appears elsewhere.

Today I passed a public place where a number of people had collected. They were shouting abuse and accusations against the authorities for not taking any notice of legitimate complaints. If they are right, and the powers-that-be are so unjust, they will make no progress and get no justice. If they are wrong, they are themselves being unjust. So why do they do it?

It can only be to make themselves feel better: that is, for at least partly selfish reasons. Perhaps if they thought this through they might be able to evolve a strategy which would gain their objectives – but then, of course, how would they stimulate themselves?

Someone has just said that people should have both a sense of justice and a capacity for heroism.

This sounds well, but it ignores what is equally important: the *use* of these things.

I know, for instance, at least one man who has a profound sense of justice and a heroic capacity to overcome it.

People constantly ask for calm and comfort and for exercises and instructions. They clamour for advice and interviews.

More often than not, they are in need of something else first, which alone will make what they want possible.

If they would only ponder, they would soon see that they are rather like the traveller who wanted shade but did not realise that he had first to find a tree to provide it.

It may be unjust to expect wisdom from the foolish: but it is surely as unjust to expect the kind of foolishness which these people seek from the wise.

'When,' asked a youth of a Sufi master, 'will I be ready to plan my own studies?'

'At the precise moment,' answered the sage, 'when you have given up the idea of planning your own studies.'

My respected grandsire Jan-Fishan Khan once said:

'If you want to be owned by a tyrant, accept someone who only *imagines* that he can be a pupil.'

Every raisin may contain a pip.

Can you have butter before you milk
the cow?

The least striking words or actions of a teacher are incomparably more precious than the 'greatnesses' of anyone else.

What a lot of people call wisdom is only ignorance carried on by other methods.

It is easy to teach people how to argue. This is based on a tendency and can be developed very easily. You can even pick it up from others, given enough exposure to it.

But how and when not to argue – that you have to learn for yourself.

How sad that only hindsight proves the truth of aphorisms which one found it hard to accept many years ago.

For instance what a teacher told me over thirty years ago:

'Try to understand. If you cannot make progress in this, then obey. If you cannot obey, forget metaphysics altogether, for there is no alternative to either of these paths.'

Nothing is ever lost while even a single person remains to remind us of it.

Anyone who says or writes anything which seems to conflict with the true or false beliefs of a community or any part of it deliberately accepts the risk of being misunderstood and vilified and perhaps punished. People are widely held to have the right to attack what they dislike. We have not yet, however, reached the stage where it is required that people understand (though they purport to describe) the roots of liking and of disliking.

If writers were emperors of the world, I know what they would do first. They would make it a capital offence for anyone to say, ever again, either 'So you're a writer? Had anything published yet?'; or 'I have a great idea for a bestseller, I'll just tell you, and you write it up for us, will you?'

Our great Teacher Bahaudin Naqshband of Bokhara, on vanity:

'Vanity is that disease of the human whose first and major symptom is to blind the afflicted to its presence. Its second and other powerful symptom is to make the patient accuse others of vanity, while believing that himself shows every sign of modesty.'

People think that anything that amazes them must be important. The Sufi's task, however, is to stress the difference between the unusual and the significant.

Some people rush so much that they would, if they could, get to Wednesday before Monday.

Try always to do what you *wish*, and you will often sacrifice what you *can* do.

A man I met at a reception in London said: 'I am an expert on Idries Shah. Now I'd like to tell you all about him...'

He didn't understand what I was on about when I replied: 'No, don't tell me all about him, just where he is at the moment.'

Another man, also recently encountered, was wearing clerical attire. I asked him what its purpose was. 'Well, you see,' he explained, 'if the Lord were to come back to Earth, he would know that I was his servant.'

Think about it – I still am...

You asked why a teacher should have described you as 'an idiot'.

I can only say that it is for the same reason that a thermometer may describe a fever as '104 degrees Fahrenheit'.

You really cannot unify different creeds. But you can disunify what lies beyond all of them.

People love to coin words, like 'the Zoosphere' for the kingdom of living things – so let me have my turn. To me, the totemist mentality is so widespread, whether people realise it or not, that the world should be renamed 'The Iconosphere'.

Have you heard about the man who asked a demon to help him with a certain matter?

The demon answered:

'That which is given by demons is not help. That which is help is not given by demons.'

'There is only one thing wrong with your type of religion,' said a dervish to a devotee, 'and that is that you have to become a saint before you can practise it.'

Have you ever considered the Sufi adage:

'Pointed bluntness, cold heat, long shortness all have the same meaning as wise scholar.'

A Civil Service committee was in session. A man called as a witness said: 'I won't talk!'

The Chairman asked:

'What does he say?'

The witness's lawyer stood up. 'My client said that he has an ongoing non-verbalisation capability at this moment in time.'

'That's better,' said the Chairman.

The key to what human beings are doing really is that they are looking for excitement. I cherish the indignation with which someone once said to me: 'You are looking at me with a calmness bordering on the insulting.'

Someone asked me just now which Eastern saying the West is in most need of.

How about: 'If you have two shirts, sell one and buy a rose'?

I used to quote much that I learnt, when a thinker said to me:

'You are fond of quoting Kurdish, Tibetan and Armenian proverbs, my friend. My counsel is that you first look at what actually happened to all those peoples.'

Simplicity is more complicated than it looks.

One of the world's greatest thinkers, such was his repute, telephoned me saying that he wanted to bring a 'Man of Wisdom' to see me.

I couldn't help saying that if the gentleman really was a man of wisdom, he would be unlikely to need to see me. If, on the other hand, he was not, I did not feel like seeing him.

That was some time ago, and the Great Thinker is now dead. But for years afterwards, people would tell me how, after that conversation, he flew into a towering rage every time he heard my name.

What is the value of the husk, once the seed has sprouted?

The lightest word of a teacher is more valuable than people realise: a bird dropped a feather and a hundred ants found shelter beneath it.

Look at all the water trapped in an iceberg. Can you drink until it is melted?

I don't claim to have originated this phrase or even to subscribe unreservedly to its implications, but you might like to know that there is a current saying in the Middle East:

'Those whom God desires to drive mad, he first makes into Orientalists!'

It used to be considered profound to say: 'Tell it like it is' – until someone noted that if you can tell it at all – it isn't like that at all.

Before you accept an offered kindness, reflect whether you will one day be reminded of it.

People are always wondering why the piling of fact on fact, from all sorts of sources, carried on by some researchers, yields so little. I can only quote the saying: 'You can never find out the time in a clock shop.'

I can well imagine that few things would have delighted Sheikh Abdul-Qadir Gilani, the great Sufi, more than a recent historian's assertion that 'there is no evidence that he ever really existed'.

Today I spoke to a man who was newly released from hospital after (as he put it) 'being driven crazy by a Spiritual Teacher'.

I asked him whether he had noticed anything unusual about the revered mentor's followers before he joined the cult.

'Oh, yes,' he said, 'but I had read in a London Sunday newspaper historical survey that very many of the early Christians appeared to their contemporaries to be completely mad. In fact, I doubt whether my late mentor has driven anything like as many people mad as at least some larger and more established systems regularly do, with little or no criticism of them.'

Ordinary life and conventionally evaluated experience is not so much a delusion as the father of a delusion. That delusion is that nothing equally important exists beyond it.

A couple of decades ago an influential Western politician came to see me. This week we met again, and he said that he would visit me once more.

I looked up the note which I had made the first time. He had said: 'You people from undeveloped countries, with no experience or responsibility in world affairs, have not the moral authority of a country like ours, with its world role and industrial future.'

I was curious to know what his ideas would be like, and when he came here yesterday I asked him to tape-record a summary of his feelings on the subject of moral authority without mentioning my diary entry.

This is what he has drafted on a piece of paper and read out; worth preserving because he is now ranked as one of the great contemporary world statesmen:

'Now that we can see the futility of infinite technological expansion; now that our country can no longer be accused of harbouring expansionist aims, it is we who have the moral authority to tell the other countries that their way should be towards low-level technology, even if it means a poorer life...'

What you put in the pot, they say, is
what your ladle brings out.

HUMAN BEINGS: *Operating Instructions:*

1. Activate Brain.
2. Operate Tongue, writing hand, etc. Considerable practice is necessary for best results.

Caution! Operating in reverse order often causes irreparable damage to the individual, to the environment and to associated systems.

In case of malfunction – RUN!

Repairs and Adjustments: Your friendly neighbourhood repairman can usually do nothing, but since nobody believes this, everyone can have a lot of fun. By the time the facts are discovered it is generally too late for anyone to have to take the blame.

Replacements and Spares: Not recommended.

Durability: Maximum possible under existing circumstances.

Attention: All it can get.

Emotion clouding judgement: YES.

Greed is the punishment of the foolish. Foolishness is the punishment of the greedy. To escape from this vicious circle, you have to work on both ends of the problem.

You say that although you do not know or practise it, you recommend it to others. But, surely, there can be only two possible descriptions of those who sell lanterns to the blind: knaves or fools?

The complaint, made at a semi-public dinner by a university dignitary about me, I am told, should be endured in silence. If it were entirely personal, I would agree wholeheartedly with this advice. But the learned gentleman has represented his criticism as a judgement of Sufis, and therefore it is useful to inform him and others what the Sufi attitude is towards his outburst. Briefly, he feels rejected. He is on record as having said that 'even Kings have been pleased to accept the honorary Doctorate of this University. Idries Shah alone, showing Sufi hauteur, has seen fit to spurn our offer.'

This is what really happened. I was told that I was to be offered an honorary Doctorate by that University. I was asked whether I would be available to accept the honour. A copy of the encomium to be read on the occasion was enclosed with the letter containing this information. I had to decline partly because doctorates had been awarded for theses which were based only on outward observations of Sufis or supposed Sufis, by that University. Further, the citation in my case claimed that I had helped to further this process. Now, if a credential in jam-making were to be offered to someone who had simply observed jam externally, what would that recommendation be worth in the eyes of tasters of jam, let alone makers of it or others who had actually participated? I rejected the phrase, 'the ultimate legitimisation of Sufism as a branch of study' as a distortion. If this is 'Sufi hauteur', so be it. But what is it to be called when none of the points which I have here brought out is mentioned by the illustrious academic who accuses me – or us? Not censorship or selective quotation, surely?

When you know enough about your own thinking, you can judge the quality of others' assessments of it. You might be surprised to find how many people ascribe your dishonesty to stupidity, and what is only your foolishness to evil intent.

Beware, certainly, of whomever tries to deceive you.

Be even more wary, though, if you are tempted to deceive others, or yourself.

The beginning for the Traveller on the Path is to start to look for faults in himself which he previously sought in others; and to begin to perceive in others the merits which he formerly imagined to be his own.

Envy is an upside-down condition, in which the lesser sees the greater as lesser: and the greater may treat the lesser as greater.

When will it become forbidden to forbid?

Have you noticed how many worthless comments begin with the words 'This is worthless'?

Whoever really knows how to hide himself need never assume disguise, lock a door or find a secret place.

Whoever knows how to reveal himself also knows when and where to do so.

You say that you do not want to know what you have decided to seek, but what you need to know.

That is a very good beginning. It avoids, for example, the problem of the farmer who wanted to control the growth of his crops and, when his wish was granted, modified the wind and the rain. But he got no yield, because he had no knowledge of the minerals in the soil.

In doing my human duty to the utmost, I am indulging in the highest form of selfishness. That is, as someone remarked to me recently, 'You may be a martyr in putting up with me, but ultimately you are doing it for yourself!'

But the matter goes further than that. I can't forget that when I was in a similar position, whatever my teacher was deriving from enduring me, only started to progress when I could feel and express both obedience and gratitude.

Only the flavour of real obedience and real gratitude can fuel the progress of human beings. That is why hypocrites and theoreticians are so far from understanding so much.

Whoever never says 'I am ignorant' is not only not a teacher, such a person has never even been a learner.

Overheard at a party: 'I don't think that psychology has actually killed Christianity. But it certainly has hit it over the head!'

Wisdom can feel and understand what folly cannot see or even imagine.

For every person who writes a book, there are a thousand readers of books. Everyone knows that there are bad writers. But there are also bad readers; people who waste their own efforts and those of writers by imagining that literacy and a desire to consume are a sufficient preparation for reading; and that highly selective reading or absorption of this or that is 'specialisation'.

One of the most important human tasks is to realise how often one is being emotional when one thinks the feeling is 'spiritual', and how frequently people who think that they are being 'good' are simply being hypocritical.

People are always asking the difference between spiritual groups and teaching bodies in the same field. What a pity that they usually don't want to hear the answer. This can be rendered through the ancient Chinese saying: 'Give me a fish and you give me a meal. Teach me to fish and you feed me for a lifetime.'

People go to supposedly spiritual groups and get a kind of nourishment which they rightly (but sometimes too stridently) insist is of value. But they have to return again and again. This is 'being given the fish'. If they were 'taught how to fish' – helped with the means to spiritual understanding – *that* would be progress.

Among the Sufis, it is worth noting, the 'spiritual experience' is the mark of the beginner, as the classical writings attest.

The adventures of Sufis are not to be found only in remote Asia and ancient times. Recently a Sufi who had agreed to give a talk in a certain town in the West arrived at the railway station and looked for a taxi to take him to the hall where he was to speak.

He found a railway porter and asked him to call a cab, for the time was getting short and the hall was far away.

'I am afraid that I can't do that,' said the porter, 'you see, there's an important lecture being given tonight, and all the taxis have been booked for weeks...'

There are two chief forms of laziness:

1. Not doing what one can;
2. Doing only what one wants to do.

The truth may hurt, the lie may please. Should you therefore avoid the one and adopt the other? Certainly – if you are working only in the field of social relationships.

There are six stages in Sufi development which may be perceived through words:

First, a man asks what a Sufi is; second, he says that he need not be a Sufi; third, he wants to become a Sufi; fourth, he says that he *is* a Sufi; fifth, he says that he is not a Sufi; sixth, he arrives at the point when he can say that he is a Sufi again – but he does not want to say it...

You are the guardian of your secret.
Reveal it, and you become its prisoner.

People become disgruntled when they insist, inwardly, on regarding themselves as consumers and when you do not allow them to consume (because you realise that they need not be constantly infantile) or because they don't recognise consumption in all its aspects.

When I was a small boy a Sufi took me to a football game and told me to study how the teams trained for their matches.

He said:

'One day you will visit the countries where this game was originally developed. You will be amazed that the people there have forgotten in many subjects that to get the fruits of a study they must respect, obey and follow its established patterns. Those who can recall this or who can learn it anew will be able to find what they need. Most of them, however, want the goal but try to ignore the prior need for method. Since the instructor knows the method, we respect him over all others. Seek such people as I have mentioned. Most of those who seek you, however, will be the others.'

Your remark is impressive, but valuable – if at all – only to yourself: like meditating naked on the roof on a cold, wet night.

Remove desire from thought, and you will have understanding.

Those who have no hope can easily find some: it comes of itself, through patience.

A mind without inner knowledge is a body without food.

Anger and placidity are both first signs of madness.

It is not for nothing that the tongue is a prisoner in the mouth.

To refuse to learn is aggression against oneself.

When you are ignorant, cynicism or suspicion are diseases.

If you must envy, envy the good – if your desire is granted, you will be cured.

A Sufi was asked: 'Is there any good which people do not crave, or any evil not to be forgiven?'

He said:

'Yes. The first is humility, the second is pride.'

If you really know the branch, you know the root.

A Request

If you enjoyed this book, please review it on Amazon and Goodreads.

Reviews are an author's best friend.

To stay in touch with news on forthcoming editions of Idries Shah works, please sign up for the mailing list:

http://bit.ly/ISFlist

And to follow him on social media, please go to any of the following links:

https://twitter.com/idriesshah

https://www.facebook.com/IdriesShah

http://www.youtube.com/idriesshah999

http://www.pinterest.com/idriesshah/

http://bit.ly/ISgoodreads

http://idriesshah.tumblr.com

https://www.instagram.com/idriesshah/

http://idriesshahfoundation.org

www.ingramcontent.com/pod-product-compliance
Lightning Source LLC
Chambersburg PA
CBHW021124020426
42331CB00005B/625